THE TRUTH ABOUT EARLY AMERICAN HISTORY

THE TRUTH ABOUT THE CONSTITUTIONAL CONVENTION

CHARLOTTE TAYLOR

Please visit our website, www.enslow.com. For a free color catalog of all our high-quality books, call toll free 1-800-398-2504 or fax 1-877-980-4454.

Library of Congress Cataloging-in-Publication Data

Names: Taylor, Charlotte, author.
Title: The truth about the Constitutional Convention / Charlotte Taylor.
Description: New York : Enslow Publishing, 2023. | Series: The truth about early American history | Title from cover. | Includes bibliographical references and index.
Identifiers: LCCN 2022000287 (print) | LCCN 2022000288 (ebook) | ISBN 9781978527928 (library binding) | ISBN 9781978527904 (paperback) | ISBN 9781978527911 (set) | ISBN 9781978527935 (ebook)
Subjects: LCSH: United States. Constitutional Convention (1787)–Juvenile literature. | United States. Constitution–Juvenile literature. | United States–Politics and government–1783-1789–Juvenile literature. | Constitutional history–United States–Juvenile literature.
Classification: LCC E303 .T347 2023 (print) | LCC E303 (ebook) | DDC 973.3-dc23/eng/20220111
LC record available at https://lccn.loc.gov/2022000287
LC ebook record available at https://lccn.loc.gov/2022000288

Published in 2023 by
Enslow Publishing
29 E. 21st Street
New York, NY 10010

Copyright © 2023 Enslow Publishing

Portions of this work were originally authored by Barbara M. Linde and published as *Thomas Jefferson Didn't Sign the Constitution: Exposing Myths About the Constitutional Convention*. All new material in this edition was authored by Charlotte Taylor.

Designer: Rachel Rising
Editor: Megan Quick

Photo credits: Cover Ian Dagnall / Alamy Stock Photo; Cover, pp. 1-6, 8, 10, 12-15, 18, 20, 22-24, 26, 28, 30-32 iulias/Shutterstock.com; Cover, pp. 1-6, 8, 10, 12-15, 18, 20, 22-24, 26, 28, 30-32 orangeberry/Shutterstock.com; Cover, Brian A Jackson/Shutterstock.com; Cover, pp. 1-6, 8,10, 12-15, 18, 20, 22, 24, 26 , 28, 30-32 pashabo/Shutterstock.com; Cover, pp. 1, 3, 5, 6, 8, 10, 13, 15, 16, 18, 20, 22, 24, 26, 28, 30-32 Epifantsev/Shutterstock.com; p. 4 eurobanks/Shutterstock.com; p. 5 James Steidl/Shutterstock.com; p. 7 Pictures Now / Alamy Stock Photo; p. 9 North Wind Picture Archives / Alamy Stock Photo; p. 11 https://commons.wikimedia.org/wiki/File:Joseph_Siffrein_Duplessis_-_Benjamin_Franklin_-_Google_Art_Project.jpg; p. 12 https://commons.wikimedia.org/wiki/File:Official_Presidential_portrait_of_Thomas_Jefferson_(by_Rembrandt_Peale,_1800)(cropped).jpg; p. 13 https://commons.wikimedia.org/wiki/File:James_Madison_by_Gilbert_Stuart.jpg; p. 14 https://commons.wikimedia.org/wiki/File:George_Mason.jpg; p. 15 https://commons.wikimedia.org/wiki/File:AdoptionOf13thAmendment.jpg; p. 17 Andrey_Popov/Shutterstock.com; p. 19 s_oleg/Shutterstock.com; p. 19 https://en.wikipedia.org/wiki/File:Constitution_of_the_United_States,_page_1.jpg; p. 21 mark reinstein/Shutterstock.com; p.23 Honey Maple/Shutterstock.com; p. 23 robuart/Shutterstock.com; p. 23 VectorsMarket/Shutterstock.com; p. 23 Pro Symbols/Shutterstock.com; p. 23 Chris Bain/Shutterstock.com; p. 23 https://commons.wikimedia.org/wiki/File:Seal_of_the_United_States_House_of_Representatives.svg; p. 23 https://commons.wikimedia.org/wiki/File:Seal_of_the_United_States_Senate.svg; p. 25 Everett Collection/Shutterstock.com; p. 27 Jack R Perry Photography/Shutterstock.com; p. 29 https://commons.wikimedia.org/wiki/File:Foundation_of_the_American_Government_by_Henry_Hintermeister.jpg.

All rights reserved. No part of this book may be reproduced in any form without permission in writing from the publisher, except by a reviewer.

Printed in the United States of America

Some of the images in this book illustrate individuals who are models. The depictions do not imply actual situations or events.

CPSIA compliance information: Batch #CSENS23: For further information contact Enslow Publishing, New York, New York, at 1-800-398-2504.

Find us on

CONTENTS

FROM COLONIES TO A COUNTRY 4

CREATING THE CONSTITUTION 6

THE DELEGATES 8

FAMILIAR FACES................................. 10

JEFFERSON'S PART 12

THE CONSTITUTION AND SLAVERY 14

VOTING RIGHTS 16

FAMOUS FIRST WORDS......................... 18

DEMOCRACY OR REPUBLIC? 20

MADISON MAKES HIS MARK.................. 22

TIME TO SIGN 24

DIVIDED STATES 26

THE CHANGING CONSTITUTION 28

GLOSSARY 30

FOR MORE INFORMATION 31

INDEX.. 32

WORDS IN THE GLOSSARY APPEAR IN **BOLD** TYPE
THE FIRST TIME THEY ARE USED IN THE TEXT.

FROM COLONIES TO A COUNTRY

The area that would become the United States went through many changes in the 1700s. It began as 13 colonies that were ruled by England. The colonies fought a war against England to become independent. Afterward, they could finally create their own government.

The United States observes Constitution Day on September 17. This is the day when **delegates** to the Constitutional Convention signed the document in 1787.

In 1787, a group of delegates met in Philadelphia, Pennsylvania, to make decisions about the United States government. This gathering became the Constitutional **Convention**. Today, some facts about the U.S. Constitution's history have become mixed up or forgotten. Let's learn the truth about how this important American **document** was created.

Explore More!

MANY COUNTRIES HAVE SOME TYPE OF WRITTEN CONSTITUTION THAT EXPLAINS HOW THEIR GOVERNMENT IS SET UP. OTHERS DO NOT HAVE ONE AT ALL. THE U.S. CONSTITUTION IS ONE OF THE OLDEST STILL IN USE. PEOPLE FROM MANY COUNTRIES HAVE USED IT AS A MODEL WHEN WRITING THEIR OWN.

CREATING THE CONSTITUTION

The Constitutional Convention began on May 25, 1787, in Philadelphia. Some delegates simply wanted to fix the set of laws that the states already had in place. These laws were called the Articles of Confederation. But many delegates did not like the Articles. They wanted to start fresh.

Under the Articles of Confederation, the United States' national government had little power. The delegates in Philadelphia decided to make the government stronger. They also needed to make new laws. They worked from May to September, through a long, hot summer. After a lot of arguing, the delegates had created a new government.

EXPLORE MORE!

THE ORIGINAL U.S. CONSTITUTION CONTAINS ABOUT 4,500 WORDS, NOT INCLUDING THE **SIGNATURES** OR THE BILL OF RIGHTS. THIS MAKES IT ONE OF THE SHORTEST WRITTEN CONSTITUTIONS IN THE WORLD. TO COMPARE, THE LONGEST IS INDIA'S, WHICH HAS MORE THAN 146,000 WORDS.

This painting shows the delegates at the Constitutional Convention. They are sometimes known as framers because they framed, or built, the Constitution.

THE DELEGATES

Each of the 13 states had the chance to send delegates to the Constitutional Convention. However, one state did not take part: Rhode Island. Many of its people liked being independent. They were afraid that a stronger **federal** government would have too much power over their small state.

The rest of the states chose 70 delegates in all, and 55 attended the convention. The framers were all well-educated white men who owned land and were leaders in their own states. They also had strong opinions and very different ideas about how to form the new government.

EXPLORE MORE!

BY 1787, THE UNITED STATES WAS IN TROUBLE. AFTER THE AMERICAN REVOLUTION, THE COUNTRY WAS IN **DEBT**. STATES WERE FIGHTING WITH EACH OTHER FOR MONEY AND POWER. DELEGATES AT THE CONSTITUTIONAL CONVENTION HOPED TO BRING THE STATES TOGETHER UNDER A NEW CENTRAL GOVERNMENT.

FAMILIAR FACES

The U.S. Constitution was created about 11 years after the Declaration of Independence was adopted. Many people think that the same group of men worked on both documents. In fact, only six of the Founding Fathers had active roles in both events.

Some important figures did not take part in the convention because they weren't in favor of a stronger federal government. A few Founding Fathers, such as Samuel Adams and Patrick Henry, chose not to attend. They worried that the new constitution would not do enough to protect the rights of individual citizens.

EXPLORE MORE!

GEORGE WASHINGTON SUCCESSFULLY LED THE MILITARY IN THE AMERICAN REVOLUTION. AFTER THE WAR, HE HOPED TO LIVE QUIETLY ON HIS LARGE FARM IN VIRGINIA. INSTEAD, HE WAS TALKED INTO ATTENDING THE CONSTITUTIONAL CONVENTION. HE BECAME ITS LEADER. TWO YEARS LATER, HE WAS ELECTED PRESIDENT OF THE UNITED STATES.

Benjamin Franklin was the most famous Founding Father to sign both the Declaration of Independence and the U.S. Constitution.

JEFFERSON'S PART

One of the most well-known Founding Fathers, Thomas Jefferson, was not present at the Constitutional Convention. Many people suppose that he was there because he was the main writer of the Declaration of Independence. However, Jefferson was the U.S. **ambassador** to France at the time and lived in Paris.

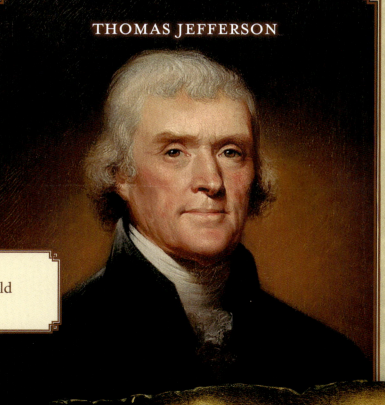

THOMAS JEFFERSON

James Madison assured the delegates at the convention that Thomas Jefferson would adopt the Constitution if he were present.

In spite of this, Jefferson still played a part in the convention. He shared his ideas about the Constitution in letters to his close friend James Madison. He also sent Madison books about laws and governments. Madison used the books as he helped to write the Constitution.

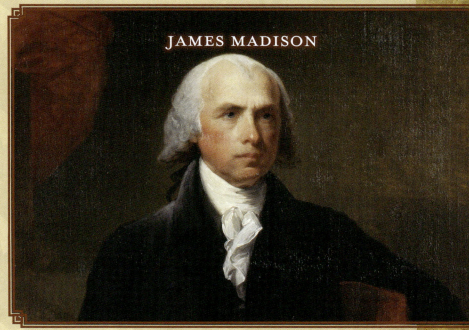

JAMES MADISON

EXPLORE MORE!

LIKE SOME OTHER FOUNDING FATHERS, JEFFERSON WAS WORRIED THAT THE CONSTITUTION GAVE THE GOVERNMENT TOO MUCH POWER. HE BELIEVED THE DOCUMENT NEEDED AN ADDITION THAT LISTED THE RIGHTS OF ALL CITIZENS. JAMES MADISON USED SOME OF HIS FRIEND'S IDEAS WHEN HE WROTE THE BILL OF RIGHTS IN 1789.

THE CONSTITUTION AND SLAVERY

The word "slavery" is not in the main Constitution. It would be easy to conclude that no one talked about the subject at the convention. This is not true. The delegates argued about slavery for months. Many opposed it. But people in the South believed their **economy** depended on crops that enslaved people were forced to produce. To get southern support, the framers of the Contitution **compromised**.

George Mason was a convention delegate who spoke strongly against slavery. However, he kept many enslaved people on his own large farm.

First, they agreed that Congress wouldn't ban trade in enslaved people from Africa until 1808. Enslaved people seeking freedom could be caught in the North and returned to the South. Last, three-fifths of enslaved people would be counted as part of each state's population. This gave southern states more **representatives** in government.

EXPLORE MORE!

THERE HAVE BEEN 27 AMENDMENTS, OR OFFICIAL CHANGES, MADE TO THE ORIGINAL CONSTITUTION. THE 13TH AMENDMENT, PASSED IN 1865, FINALLY PUT AN END TO THE PRACTICE OF SLAVERY IN ALL STATES. IT CAME AT THE END OF THE U.S. CIVIL WAR.

VOTING RIGHTS

The right to vote is a key part of being an American citizen. It would make sense that the framers of the Constitution would include rules about it when they created the new government. They did not! Instead, they gave the states the right to decide who could vote.

In the early days of the United States, only white men who owned land were regularly able to vote. In 1870, the 15th Amendment gave Black men the right to vote. Women couldn't vote until the 19th Amendment was approved in 1920. Native Americans weren't allowed to vote until 1924 (and some states didn't allow them to vote until even later).

EXPLORE MORE!

THE 15TH AMENDMENT GAVE BLACK MEN THE RIGHT TO VOTE, BUT SOME STATES STILL MADE IT VERY HARD FOR THEM. SPECIAL TAXES, READING TESTS, AND THREATS KEPT MANY BLACK MEN FROM CASTING VOTES. IN SOME AREAS, THIS LASTED UNTIL THE CIVIL RIGHTS MOVEMENT OF THE 1960S.

The voting age in the United States was 21 until the 26th Amendment was passed in 1971. It allows U.S. citizens to vote at age 18.

FAMOUS FIRST WORDS

The Constitution is a very famous document, but many people still get the words wrong. One of the most common misunderstandings is that it states that "all men are created equal." These words are actually in the first part of the Declaration of Independence: "We hold these truths to be self-evident, that all men are created equal."

The famous opening of the Constitution is "We the People of the United States." This was actually a late change. At first, it read: "We the people of the States of New Hampshire, Massachusetts, ..." It listed all 13 states!

EXPLORE MORE!

THE ORIGINAL HANDWRITTEN CONSTITUTION CONTAINS A FEW MISTAKES. THE MOST NOTICEABLE ONE WAS MADE BY ALEXANDER HAMILTON. AS HE RECORDED THE NAMES OF THE DELEGATES' STATES, HE WROTE "PENNSYLVANIA" WITH ONE N INSTEAD OF TWO. THE ERROR IS STILL ON THE DOCUMENT TODAY.

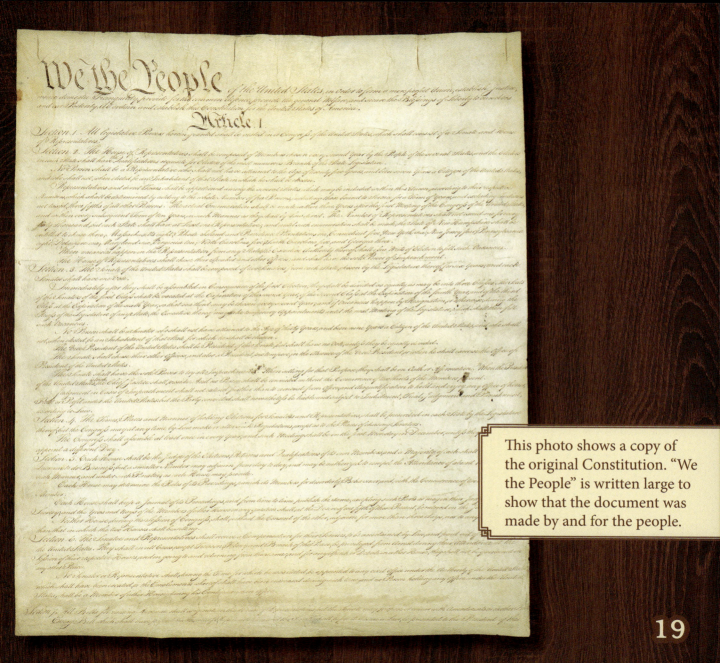

This photo shows a copy of the original Constitution. "We the People" is written large to show that the document was made by and for the people.

DEMOCRACY OR REPUBLIC?

A democracy is a government in which every citizen has a voice. This is true in the United States. However, the Constitution does not state that the nation is a democracy. The framers called their new government a republic.

In a democracy, the **majority** rules. This worried the delegates. They did not want one group to have too much power. In a republic, people choose representatives to decide most matters in government. A set of laws, such as a constitution, prevents the government from taking away the rights of all people.

EXPLORE MORE!

IDEAS ABOUT THE U.S. GOVERNMENT HAVE CHANGED OVER THE YEARS. TODAY, THE UNITED STATES IS OFTEN CALLED A DEMOCRATIC REPUBLIC. IT IS A DEMOCRACY BECAUSE THE PEOPLE HAVE THE POWER, AND IT IS A REPUBLIC BECAUSE THEY ELECT GOVERNMENT REPRESENTATIVES.

Americans elect members of Congress to represent them in Washington, DC.

MADISON MAKES HIS MARK

James Madison presented the Virginia Plan at the Constitutional Convention. It called for a strong central government with three branches. Much of his proposal was used, and he is called the Father of the Constitution. Stories say Madison wrote much of the document. However, this is a mix of myth and fact.

Madison did play a major role at the convention. But George Washington was the president of the convention. Gouverneur Morris wrote much of the final document. Roger Sherman helped the large and small states reach a compromise. In Madison's words, the Constitution was "the work of many heads and many hands."

EXPLORE MORE!

EVERY DAY DURING THE CONVENTION, JAMES MADISON TOOK NOTES—LOTS OF THEM. THEY ARE THE BEST RECORD THAT EXISTS OF THE CONVENTION, WHICH TOOK PLACE IN SECRET. HE ORDERED THE NOTES NOT TO BE MADE PUBLIC UNTIL EVERY DELEGATE HAD DIED.

THE THREE BRANCHES OF THE U.S. GOVERNMENT

LEGISLATIVE

MAKES THE LAWS

CONGRESS

House of Representatives

Senate

EXECUTIVE

CARRIES OUT THE LAWS

president → vice president

↓

many government departments and agencies

JUDICIAL

JUDGES THE LAWS

federal / state courts

The Constitution set up the government with three branches, as James Madison suggested.

23

TIME TO SIGN

The Constitutional Convention lasted for four months, and not every delegate stayed for the entire event. Some left early for business, while a few others became sick. Therefore, not all 55 delegates signed the Constitution. It's commonly said that 39 men signed the document. But that's only partly true.

There are 40 signatures on the Constitution. William Jackson was the convention secretary, but he was not a delegate. He took notes and made sure the meetings were secret. Jackson signed the Constitution, but he isn't considered an official signer.

EXPLORE MORE!

SEVERAL OF THE 55 DELEGATES DID NOT SIGN BECAUSE THEY WERE UNHAPPY WITH THE CONSTITUTION. GEORGE MASON, EDMUND RANDOLPH, ELBRIDGE GERRY, AND OTHERS TOOK PART IN THE CONVENTION, BUT THEY REFUSED TO SIGN BECAUSE THERE WAS NO BILL OF RIGHTS.

done in Convention by the Unanimous
Day of September in the Year of our Lord one
of the Independance of the United States of
We have hereunto subscribed our Names,

The signatures on the Constitution were grouped by state. Ben Franklin, who represented Pennsylvania, was the oldest delegate and needed help signing.

DIVIDED STATES

Once the Constitution was written, each state needed to **ratify** it. After months of talks and compromises, you might expect that the people of the states were fairly happy with the document and ready to approve it. In fact, a large group of people still had doubts.

People called the Federalists supported the Constitution. Others, called Anti-Federalists, thought it made the federal government too strong. Federalists promised a bill of rights would be added to the Constitution. Knowing the federal government's powers would be limited eased some people's fears about the Constitution.

EXPLORE MORE!

ONLY NINE OF THE 13 STATES NEEDED TO RATIFY THE CONSTITUTION IN ORDER FOR IT BECOME LAW. ON JUNE 21, 1788, NEW HAMPSHIRE BECAME THE NINTH STATE TO RATIFY THE DOCUMENT. RHODE ISLAND WAS THE LAST ORIGINAL STATE TO RATIFY, ON MAY 29, 1790.

The Bill of Rights was ratified in 1791. It promised Americans certain rights and freedoms, such as the freedom of speech.

THE CHANGING CONSTITUTION

The United States had a population of 4 million people when the Constitution was signed. Today, the country's population is more than 330 million. The country has grown and changed, and so has the Constitution. The framers wanted it to be hard, but not impossible, to change the document. People have talked about and argued over each amendment, just like the original Constitution.

Even though there have been changes, the basic ideas of the Constitution remain. Every day, people make decisions within the system that the framers built. Learning about the Constitution and its creators is a great way to understand the U.S. government today.

EXPLORE MORE!

PEOPLE HAVE SUGGESTED MORE THAN 11,000 AMENDMENTS TO THE CONSTITUTION OVER THE YEARS. OF THOSE, ONLY 27 HAVE BEEN RATIFIED BY CONGRESS AND THE STATES.

This painting shows Gouverneur Morris signing the Constitution in front of George Washington.

GLOSSARY

ambassador: Someone sent by one group or country to speak for it in different places.

compromise: A way of two sides reaching agreement in which each gives up something to end an argument.

convention: A gathering of people who have a common interest or purpose.

debt: An amount of money owed.

delegate: A representative of one of the 13 colonies.

document: A formal piece of writing.

economy: The money made in an area and how it is made.

federal: Having to do with the national government.

majority: The group that is the greater part of a large group.

ratify: To give formal approval to something.

representative: One who stands for a group of people. A member of a lawmaking body who acts for voters.

signature: A person's name written in that person's handwriting.

FOR MORE INFORMATION

BOOKS

Lusted, Marcia Amidon. *The Bill of Rights*. North Mankato, MN: Capstone Press, 2020.

Shamir, Ruby. *What's the Big Deal About Elections*. New York, NY: Philomel Books, 2020.

Trusiani, Lisa. *The History of the Constitution*. Emeryville, CA: Rockridge Press, 2021.

WEBSITES

Ducksters: Constitution

www.ducksters.com/history/us_constitution.php

Find out more about the Constitution with fun facts and a quiz.

Kids in the House: What Is Congress?

kids-clerk.house.gov/grade-school/lesson.html?intID=1

Learn about the three branches of government and the role of each one.

National Geographic Kids: James Madison

kids.nationalgeographic.com/history/article/james-madison

Get to know the fourth U.S. president and one of the most important figures at the Constitutional Convention.

Publisher's note to educators and parents: Our editors have carefully reviewed these websites to ensure that they are suitable for students. Many websites change frequently, however, and we cannot guarantee that a site's future contents will continue to meet our high standards of quality and educational value. Be advised that students should be closely supervised whenever they access the internet.

INDEX

amendments, 15, 16, 17, 28

American Revolution, 8

Anti-Federalists, 26

Articles of Confederation, 6

Bill of Rights, 6, 13, 24, 26, 27

branches of government, 22, 23

Congress, 15, 21

Declaration of Independence, 10, 11, 12, 18

Federalists, 26

Founding Fathers, 10, 11

Franklin, Benjamin, 11, 25

Hamilton, Alexander, 18

Jefferson, Thomas, 12, 13

Madison, James, 12, 13, 22, 23

Mason, George, 14, 24

Morris, Gouverneur, 22, 29

Philadelphia, Pennsylvania, 5, 6

ratification, 26

Sherman, Roger, 22

signatures, 24, 25

slavery, 14, 15

Virginia Plan, 22

Washington, George, 10, 22